From Castles in the Clouds

By V. Gilbert Beers

Illustrated by Helen Endres

MOODY PRESS • CHICAGO

What You Will Find in This Book

Library of Congress Cataloging in Publication Data

Beers, Victor Gilbert, 1928-
   From Castles in the Clouds
   (The Muffin Family Picture Bible)

   SUMMARY: Selected Bible stories accompanied by corresponding contemporary stories involving the imaginary Muffin family.

   1. Bible stories, English. [1. Bible stories. 2. Christian life-Fiction]. I. Endres, Helen. II. Title.

ISBN:0-8024-2879-7

Printed in the United States of America

TO PARENTS AND TEACHERS

The Bible is an old Book, written about people who lived long ago and far away, people such as Noah, Abraham, and Moses. But the Bible is also a book for today—and tomorrow—with answers for every need and problem we face. The Muffin Family provides a transition between the Bible and today's reader. Bible stories are retold in the language of today, so that your child can understand what they are saying. With each Bible story is a Muffin Family story that applies the truth of that Bible story to today's living. That application is not merely a principle to learn, but also an example to follow. Thus, the Muffin Family stories are a transition from God at work in the lives of long-ago people to God at work in your life now. In previous books, the Muffin Family has compared that transition to a bridge (*Over Buttonwood Bridge*), a special tree (*Under the Tagalong Tree*), a special window (*Through Golden Windows*), and a place where sea and sky meet (*With Sails to the Wind*). In this book, they compare it to a make-believe castle in the clouds—a place where Bible and life, reality and fantasy, fun and life's values meet, an important intersection to shape the whole person for Jesus.

MOSES-THE PRINCE WHO RAN AWAY

Slaves in a Strange Land
EXODUS 1

"Joseph?" Pharaoh roared. "Who cares about Joseph?"

Pharaoh's officers looked at each other with surprise. Almost every Egyptian remembered what a good governor Joseph had been. Joseph had stored grain during the seven years when crops were good. Later, during the seven years when crops would not grow, the Egyptians had plenty to eat while others starved.

But now Joseph was dead. The pharaoh who had made Joseph governor was dead also. The new pharaoh did not want his people to remember how great Joseph was. He wanted them to think how great and powerful he was.

The new pharaoh could not hurt Joseph now. But he could hurt Joseph's people, the Hebrews.

"There are too many of those people," said Pharaoh. "What if we should have a war? The Hebrews might fight against us."

Pharaoh began to worry about the Hebrews. He must do something about them. He must show everyone that he was more powerful than Joseph and his people.

"But how?" he asked his officers.

"Make them your slaves," an officer said.

Pharaoh liked the idea. So he ordered his officers to make the Hebrews his slaves.

The Egyptian masters were cruel to the Hebrew slaves. They forced them to carry heavy burdens and work long hours.

"Now they are tired slaves," an officer told Pharaoh. "Tired slaves do not fight against Pharaoh."

"That is true," said Pharaoh. "But there are still too many of them. What can we do about that?"

"Make them work even harder," said the officers. "Then many of them will die."

Pharaoh ordered the slave masters to be even more cruel to the Hebrews. The Hebrew slaves made bricks under the blazing sun and built cities for Pharaoh. But the work was so hard and the sun so hot that many of them died.

Pharaoh was pleased. Now everyone would know how powerful he was. They would think that he was greater than Joseph or his people, the Hebrews.

"But there are still too many Hebrews," Pharaoh told his officers. "What shall we do now? We must cause more Hebrews to die."

Pharaoh did not want his officers themselves to murder the Hebrews. That would not look good. Instead, they should find ways to make more Hebrews die, or to make the Hebrews kill their own people.

"I have a plan," said an officer. "Command the Hebrew midwives to kill all the new baby boys. We do not have to kill them ourselves. We can make them do it."

"That's it!" Pharaoh shouted. "Bring the Hebrew midwives here!" So the officers brought the midwives, the women who helped the Hebrew mothers when they had their babies.

"I command you to kill every Hebrew baby boy as soon as he is born," said Pharaoh.

The midwives listened to Pharaoh, but they would not do what he commanded. They were afraid that God would punish them if they did.

Soon Pharaoh realized that his plan was not working. He must try something else.

"We will kill the Hebrew baby boys ourselves!" he shouted. Then he ordered his officers to throw the babies into the Nile River where they would drown or be eaten by crocodiles.

So things grew worse than ever for the Hebrews. They must have thought that God had gone away and left them.

If only God would send someone to lead us from our slavery, they must have thought.

How could they know that the new baby boy in the home of Amram and Jochebed would not be thrown into the river? How could they know that instead he would grow up in Pharaoh's own house? And how could they know that some day he would lead the Hebrew people from their slavery?

Because they did not know, they prayed and waited. And while they waited, they wondered if God was listening.

WHAT DO YOU THINK?

1. How would your life have been different if you and your family had been slaves in Egypt at that time? What are some things you might have done each day?

2. What would you have thought as you waited for God to send someone to lead you from slavery? What would you have thought as the days went by and nothing happened? Would you, too, have wondered if God was listening?

From Castles in the Clouds

"That's the biggest and best castle on the whole beach," Maxi boasted.

"Maxi Muffin," said Mini. "You shouldn't brag like that. Let someone else do it."

"Well?" said Maxi.

"Well, it is a GOR-jus castle," said Mini. "And just look at all those cute little kings and queens and knights."

Mini pointed to some sticks that Maxi had poked into the sand next to his castle.

"But it isn't the BIGGEST and BEST castle," Mini said, almost a little snobby.

"OK, then, you tell me where there's a bigger or better one," Maxi snapped.

"Up there!" said Mini, pointing to a big fluffy cloud over the water.

Maxi stared at the beautiful cloud for quite some time. "Yeah," he said at last. "It does look like a big cloud castle."

Maxi and Mini lay on the beach for a long time, watching the beautiful cloud castle but saying nothing. At last Maxi had an idea.

"I wish God would send a knight out on that drawbridge and toot his horn at me."

"Maxi Muffin, you be careful what you say," said Mini. "God doesn't run around tooting at people."

"I know," said Maxi. "But I wish He would. I've been praying for something special for a long time, and He doesn't say anything. Why can't He give just one little toot to let me know it's on its way?"

"Is it?" Mini asked.

Maxi sat up and looked at Mini. He had been wondering WHEN God would send it, not IF He would.

"Suppose God doesn't want you to have this marvelous thing you want?" Mini asked. "Suppose He thinks you're not ready for it?"

"I am too!" Maxi argued.

"I didn't say you weren't ready," Mini said coolly. "I just asked what you would think if God felt you aren't ready."

Maxi tried to think of a good answer. But it wasn't as easy to argue with what God might think as it was to argue with what Mini said. Anyway Poppi had suggested that Maxi might not be ready, and Maxi thought if God and Poppi had both decided something, that was probably the way it would be.

"Well, at least He could have someone toot a big no," said Maxi. "Then I would know what to expect."

Suddenly Mini touched Maxi's arm and told him to "shush." Maxi looked everywhere to see what he was shushing for.

"Your sand king!" Mini whispered. "He's calling you. He wants you to wash the castle walls with your pail of water."

"He's kookie!" said Maxi. "His castle is made of sand. A pail of water would wreck it."

"But he WANTS it," Mini argued. "He wants you to send a sand knight to the drawbridge to toot when you're ready."

"NO! I won't do it," Maxi argued. "If he's too dumb to know what's good for him, why should I toot?"

Suddenly Maxi realized what he had said. He looked down at his sand castle. There was no knight on the drawbridge, tooting for the king who didn't know what was best for him. Then Maxi looked up at the castle in the clouds. There was no knight on that drawbridge either, tooting for Maxi.

"I guess God knows what is best for me, just like I know what is best for my sand king and his castle," Maxi whispered softly.

LET'S TALK ABOUT THIS

What this story teaches: God listens to every prayer, although at times it may seem that He doesn't. God answers in His way, although at times we may have wanted another way.

1. Why doesn't God give us whatever we want whenever we want it?
2. What did Maxi learn about the way God answers prayer? What will you remember the next time you are waiting for God to answer your prayers?

The Prince Who Ran Away
EXODUS 2:11-15

Jochebed must have often thought of how God had saved her baby boy, Moses. All the fears that Moses would be thrown into the Nile River were gone. The princess had found Moses and claimed him as her own son. She had even asked Moses' mother to nurse him.

Now Jochebed could raise Moses and teach him about God for a few years. Then he would go to the palace to live as the son of the princess.

Those were happy years for Jochebed and Amram. Nobody knows for sure how long they kept Moses in their slave hut. But even though Jochebed and Amram were still slaves, they continued to worship and thank God, for He had spared their son from death.

Jochebed must have spent many hours with her son, teaching him about their people, the Hebrews, and how God had worked in their lives. She must have told Moses about God's work in the lives of their ancestors, Abraham, Isaac, and Jacob.

Moses listened carefully to the stories about Adam and Eve, the great Flood in Noah's time, and the tower at Babel. He heard how Joseph had been sold as a slave by his brothers and had later become governor of Egypt. He must have asked many questions as Jochebed told how Joseph kept Egypt from starving and how the pharaohs who ruled later forgot Joseph and made his people slaves.

"Some day God will send a great man to free us from our slavery," Jochebed told Moses.

Perhaps the boy Moses dreamed that he might be that man. If God could cause the slave Joseph to become governor, why couldn't He cause the boy Moses to become pharaoh? And who else could free the slaves but the pharaoh?

12

At last the time came for Moses to live at the palace and be trained as a son of the princess. The best teachers taught him, the best warriors trained him to fight, and he was given the best food and clothing.

As the years passed, Moses grew to be a strong prince, admired by all who saw him. Who could ride a horse or drive a chariot better than Prince Moses? And who would dare to fight him, for he was one of the most skilled warriors in Egypt?

But even though Moses had the finest education and greatest skills in the land, he never forgot what he had learned from his mother, Jochebed. He must have often remembered the stories of his people and the way God had worked in their lives. And he must have wondered if God was preparing him to become the next pharaoh. Then he could free his people.

One day when Moses was visiting a lonely place where the Hebrew slaves were working, he saw an Egyptian taskmaster with a whip, beating a Hebrew slave. Moses became angry. As soon as the slave had run away, Moses looked this way and that to be sure no one was watching. Then he jumped from his chariot and struck the Egyptian so hard that he died.

Moses quickly buried the Egyptian in the sand and returned to the palace. He must have wondered that night if anyone had seen him, for if Pharaoh heard of it, he would surely put Moses to death.

The next day Moses returned to the same place and that time found two Hebrew slaves fighting. One was wrong, and Moses told him so.

But instead of thanking Moses for his concern, the Hebrew slave shouted angrily at him. "Who put you over us as our judge?" he growled. "Do you want to kill me as you did that Egyptian yesterday?"

The secret was out. Moses knew now that he would not be safe in Egypt, for Pharaoh would surely kill him as soon as he heard. That night, while the royal family slept, Moses slipped out of the palace and headed for Midian, a land to the east.

Thus Moses, the prince of Egypt, became Moses the runaway. No more could he dream of becoming pharaoh. No longer could he dream of leading his people from their slavery. Moses instead had to run for his life. Moses, the runaway prince, had to hide in a strange land, far from the people he had hoped to save.

WHAT DO YOU THINK?

1. One day Moses was a prince in Egypt, who might become the next pharaoh. The next day he was a runaway, headed for a foreign country to save his life. If you had been Moses running away, what are some things you might have thought about? What would you have asked God to do for you?

2. Do you think God was as near to Moses in trouble as He was when Moses had all he needed? How might Moses' prayers have been different when he was in trouble? What do you think Moses prayed for then that he did not pray for in his palace home in Egypt?

The Muffins at Moosejaw Lake

"Whew! How far is Moosejaw Lake?" Mini groaned, plopping down on a big log by the trail.

"Another fifteen minutes and we'll be there," Poppi answered. "Are you sorry we're backpacking up there?"

"I won't be when we get there," said Mini. "But we've been backpacking a hundred hours already."

"Two, to be exact," said Poppi. "But it's a special place. You won't be sorry, I'm sure."

After a short rest, the Muffins set out again, singing as they went. Ruff tried to join in the singing until Maxi and Mini shushed him for howling. Tuff wasn't along, for Poppi had said it would be a CAT-astrophe to have her on a camping trip.

Suddenly Mini stopped in the trail and gave a wild squeal. "Look!" she shouted.

Everyone looked. There through the trees they could see a little blue lake, with mountains and tall trees around it. The backpacks didn't seem heavy now as the Muffins hurried to find a place in the campground.

"Look at that!" said Poppi. "Not another person here. We're alone!"

Maxi and Mini gathered firewood, Poppi put up tents, and Mommi got the food ready for dinner. Ruff did his part by sniffing out chipmunks and barking at them.

Before long, five hungry Muffins sat around a fire, munching on dinner and watching the sun sink behind the mountains. The tall trees seemed to grow taller and taller as they became silhouettes against the sky. One by one the stars began to pop out of the sky above the trees.

"It's certainly quiet out here," Mini whispered.

"Let's all stop talking for one minute," said Poppi. "Perhaps we can hear some night sounds."

Suddenly in the distance Mini heard a "whooooo" sound. *Just an owl*, she told herself. But she did reach for Poppi's hand anyway.

Then everything was quiet for a few seconds except for the sighing sound in the tall trees and the quiet lap-lapping of the water along the shore.

Mini was listening so much for the little sounds that she wasn't ready for the screaming sound that came from across the lake. "WOLVES!" she cried out, throwing her arms around Poppi. "They're after us!"

"That's a loon," said Poppi. "Tomorrow you may see it swimming on the lake."

Mini stared up into the sky above. "I've never seen so many stars," she said. "Where did they all come from? We don't have them back home."

"They're back home, too," said Poppi. "But the bright lights of the villages and cities light up the sky too much to let us see them."

Mini looked at the bright band of stars called the Milky Way. "There are millions and millions of stars in that," she whispered.

Then Mini looked around at the tall trees. The fire was casting strange shadows upon them. Home seemed far, far away.

"Poppi, did God climb up here with us?" she asked. "Can we talk with Him here tonight, or is He down at our home?"

Poppi smiled. "He was here long before we came, Mini," he said. "He made this beautiful lake and the trees and mountains. He made the stars far out in the sky."

"Did He go away somewhere?" Mini asked.

"No, God always stays to take care of the things He makes," Poppi answered.

Then Poppi told the story of Moses, who went far from home to a strange land called Midian. He told how Moses found that God was there first, and that He was with Moses in Midian just as He had been with him in Egypt.

Mini looked at the stars. They did not seem so far away now. As she drifted off to sleep, she thought again and again, *He is here with us. He was here before we came.*

LET'S TALK ABOUT THIS

What this story teaches: Wherever we go, God has been there before we came and He remains with us.

1. Have you ever wondered if God is with you when you are far away on vacation or for some other reason? Is He?
2. How do you know that God is with you wherever you go? Why is that important?
3. Look up Jeremiah 23:23-24 in your Bible. If you memorize those verses, you will remember them when you are far from home.

In the Tents of Jethro

EXODUS 2:15—3:1

For many days Moses hurried across the hot desert sand, running away from his beautiful palace home in Egypt. He was always looking back, watching for Pharaoh's officers, for they would surely be looking for him so that they could kill him.

At last one day Moses arrived in the land of Midian. Here Pharaoh's officers could not follow. He would be safe at last.

Tired, hungry, and alone, Moses sat down by a well to think. A cool drink of water helped to revive him and give him new strength.

But Moses was troubled. Back home in Egypt he had been a prince. A prince in Egypt did not have to work for a living. Now Moses was a stranger in Midian. Now he must find a way to earn food, clothing, and a place to live.

What would he do? Where would he go now? And what would he tell these people about himself?

While Moses thought about these things, seven sisters brought their father's sheep to the well for water. But before the sisters could draw water for their sheep, some rough shepherds came with their sheep and forced the sisters to go aside so they could be first.

Moses jumped to his feet. He was angry at these rude men. Nobody would do that while he was around!

Imagine how surprised those shepherds were when one man came to fight them all. Imagine how surprised the seven sisters were when that one man taught those shepherds a lesson about fighting that they would never forget. But how could they know he was Moses, the prince who had been taught the finest skills in all Egypt?

The sisters must have been even more surprised when that mighty warrior turned back to the well and drew water for their sheep. He was not only a great fighter, but a gentle and kind man too.

Jethro, the father of the seven sisters, was surprised when his daughters returned home. "How did you finish watering the sheep so soon?" he asked. The girls were so excited they all began to tell their story at once.

"You should have seen him fight!"

"And he was so handsome."

"And an Egyptian."

"And he even watered our sheep for us!"

Jethro smiled. "Well, where is this Egyptian?" he asked. "Why did you leave him back there at the well? Now go and get him so that he may eat with us."

Nobody knows for sure how many of the seven sisters went for Moses, but they probably all did. And Moses must have smiled, too, as he was led back to the tents of Jethro by those seven happy young ladies.

Moses lived with Jethro for quite some time. The days and weeks passed into months, and Moses married Zipporah, one of the seven sisters. In time, they had a son named Gershom.

For forty years, Moses lived in Midian among Jethro's family. Moses, the prince of Egypt, was now a shepherd, quietly taking care of sheep in the desert country.

But Moses never forgot his people back in Egypt. The pharaoh who had ordered the Hebrew baby boys to be killed in time died himself. But the new pharaoh still kept the Hebrew people as his slaves.

The Hebrew slaves cried out to God for help. God remembered His promises to Abraham, Isaac, and Jacob. It was time now to raise up a man to lead His people from Egypt. That man was Moses.

So Moses, a Hebrew slave boy, had once become prince of Egypt. Then Moses, the prince of Egypt, had become a lowly shepherd of Midian. Now Moses, the lowly shepherd, was about to become God's mighty leader, a deliverer for all the people of Israel. Moses, shepherd of Jethro's flocks, was about to become a great shepherd of God's people.

WHAT DO YOU THINK?

1. How did God prepare Moses for the great work of leading His people from Egypt?

2. Do you think Moses ever dreamed of leading his people from Egypt? How did his work as a shepherd in the desert help him lead the people through the wilderness? How did his training as a prince of Egypt help?

3. Do you ever wonder what God wants you to do some day? You may not like some things you have to do now, but they may be preparing you to serve Him as you should.

School Rule

"I hate school!" Maxi Muffin announced as he slammed the front door behind him.

"Maxi!" said Mommi. "What a terrible thing to say!"

"Bad day?" asked Poppi, looking over his newspaper.

"No, well, I mean yes," said Maxi. "I did have a bad day. But I hate school even when I have a good day."

"Hmmm," said Mommi. "Last week you told me how much fun you were having."

Maxi frowned. "That was last week. This is this week."

"Have any plans?" Poppi asked quietly.

"Plans? What can I do?" asked Maxi. "I'll serve time, just like I'm in prison. What else can I do?"

"I just thought you might like to become a pirate, or a king, or even a fairy princess," Poppi said with a smile.

"Verrrry funny," Maxi answered, not at all amused by Poppi's humor. "But I'd settle for being a pilot or a banker or a policeman or a fireman."

Poppi put down his newspaper and looked at Maxi. "Tell you what I'll do," he said. "I'll call Mr. Books, your principal, to excuse you from school tomorrow. Then you and I can check out some of these jobs you would like to do."

Maxi's eyes grew wide with excitement. "Do you mean it?" he said. "That would be fun."

Early the next morning Poppi and Maxi headed out to the offices of Global Airlines. When they arrived, Poppi announced to the young lady near the door that Mr. Muffin would like to talk to the personnel manager about becoming a pilot.

Maxi and Poppi walked down two hallways and into a door marked Personnel Manager. When they came in, a smiling man stood up to shake hands.

"Now, then, Mr. Muffin," he said to Poppi. "I understand you would like to apply for a pilot's job."

"Oh, no," said Poppi. "Not I. This Mr. Muffin!" Poppi pointed to Maxi. Maxi tried to stand as tall as he could, but he felt so tiny.

"Heh, heh, is that so?" the man said with a nervous laugh.

"Yes, Poppi and I thought I might quit school so I can train to be a pilot," Maxi said bravely.

"I see," said the personnel manager. "Well, then, let's fill out this application form."

The man took a long piece of paper from his desk. "Now then, Mr. Muffin," he said to Maxi. "One of our first questions is about your education. How far have you gone?"

"Sixth grade," said Maxi, trying to stand taller than he had been.

"I'm so sorry," said the man, putting the paper back into his desk. "We will not accept applications from anyone with less than a high-school education."

"High school?" Maxi gulped.

"Plus many long months of special training," said the man.

"But why so much?" Maxi almost complained.

"How much do you want our pilots to have when they take you and your family up 36,000 feet in the air?" the man asked kindly.

Poppi and Maxi headed next for the bank downtown. But when the man in the bank asked about education, Maxi was ready to leave.

"Sorry, Maxi," said the banker. "But your Poppi and Mommi want someone handling their money who knows more than 2 + 2 = 4. Don't you, Mr. Muffin?"

Poppi nodded, and he and Maxi headed for city hall. "OK, then," said Maxi. "I'll settle for being a fireman or policeman. I'm sure they don't have to have a long time in school just to fight fires or catch crooks."

Maxi almost argued with the man at the fire department when he said, "High school education." It just didn't seem fair.

"Why?" Maxi asked. "Why do I need twelve years in school to learn to squirt water on a fire?"

The man smiled. "Our people do much more than squirt water on fires," he said. "We rescue people from burning buildings, help mommies have their babies, give artificial respiration, and many, many other things. If it were your house, or your family we were helping, what kind of fireman would you want?"

On the way to the police department, Maxi saw a policeman in the hallway. "Excuse me, sir," he said. "Do you have to have a high-school education to be a policeman?"

"Yes, you do," the policeman said. "Then we get extra training, depending on the work we do."

"Which is much more than chasing crooks," Maxi added.

The policeman smiled. "Much more," he said.

Maxi was quiet as he and Poppi drove toward home. Then he asked, "Aren't there any jobs a person can get without so much schooling?"

"Yes, there are many," said Poppi. "But you have discovered something important today, Maxi."

Maxi thought for a moment. "I guess I found out that any good work must have good preparation," Maxi said.

"Do you think that's also true of the work we do for God?" asked Poppi.

Maxi was quiet most of the way home before he answered. "I guess I learned a new rule about school," he said. "If people want me to go to school to help catch crooks and put out fires, they also expect me to prepare to do things for God."

"That's a good school rule!" said Poppi.

Then Poppi and Maxi went in to see what homework was assigned for the next day.

LET'S TALK ABOUT THIS

What this story teaches: Some things are not always fun now but may prepare us to do what God wants us to do later.

1. How do you think Moses' work with Jethro prepared him to lead the people of Israel through the wilderness?
2. How do you think your schoolwork may be preparing you to work for God later?

ELISHA-PROPHET WITH POWER

The Miracle of Oil

2 KINGS 4:1-7

In the days when Elisha was a great prophet in Israel, there was a school that trained young men to serve God. One young man attending that school borrowed some money, but before he could repay it, he died.

Now the young man's wife and two sons were in trouble. In those days, people were sold into slavery when they could not pay their debts. So when the man who had lent the money came to collect it, the young mother was terrified.

"I . . . I have no money to pay you," she said.

"Too bad!" said the man. "Then I will take your sons instead and make them my slaves."

"No, no!" the young mother cried. Then without thinking she added, "Come back tomorrow. I will have the money for you."

The man left, and the young woman began to feel a sense of panic. Where would she get the money? Why did she say that? To whom could she turn?

Then the young woman remembered Elisha, the prophet of God. He would know what to do. Leaving her two sons at home, she ran to find Elisha.

"My husband has died, and you know how he wanted to serve the Lord," she told Elisha breathlessly. "But he borrowed money so he could go to school, and now the man who lent it has come to collect. He will be there tomorrow to take my sons to be his slaves if I don't have the money. What can I do?"

"Well, what can we do?" Elisha asked. "What do you have to sell?"

"Nothing!" the woman said. "Nothing but a jar of olive oil."

"Listen carefully," Elisha told her. "Go to all your neighbors and borrow every pot that you can. Take them into your house with you and your sons and shut the door. Then pour your oil into those pots."

The woman must have wondered as she ran home. *Elisha is certainly a man of God, so he must know what God wants us to do,* she thought. *But is he saying that my one little pot of oil will fill all my neighbors' oil pots?*

She wanted to trust God to do a miracle for her. But what if that didn't work? What if she borrowed all those oil pots and then looked foolish to her friends and neighbors? No one wants to appear foolish to friends and neighbors.

Should she borrow all those pots and risk what her neighbors might think? Or should she give up and let her sons be taken as slaves?

The woman must have prayed much about that on the way home. She remembered how her husband had trusted God and how often God had helped them as her husband went to school to learn to serve Him.

By the time the woman reached home she was completely sure what she should do. "Go to all the neighbors," she told her sons. "Borrow every pot you can and bring it here."

Before long the whole house seemed to be filled with pots. There were no more pots to borrow.

The woman closed the door, as Elisha had told her to do. She and her sons were alone with a houseful of empty pots. They must have prayed earnestly for God to work the miracle Elisha had promised.

The woman's heart began to beat faster and faster as she picked up her little oil pot and began to pour. First one pot was filled, then another. The two sons stared with wide-open eyes as their mother kept on pouring oil into the third, then the fourth, and so on until every pot in the room was filled.

"Hurry, give me another pot," the woman said.

But her sons shook their heads. "There are no more," they answered. "We borrowed all we could."

30

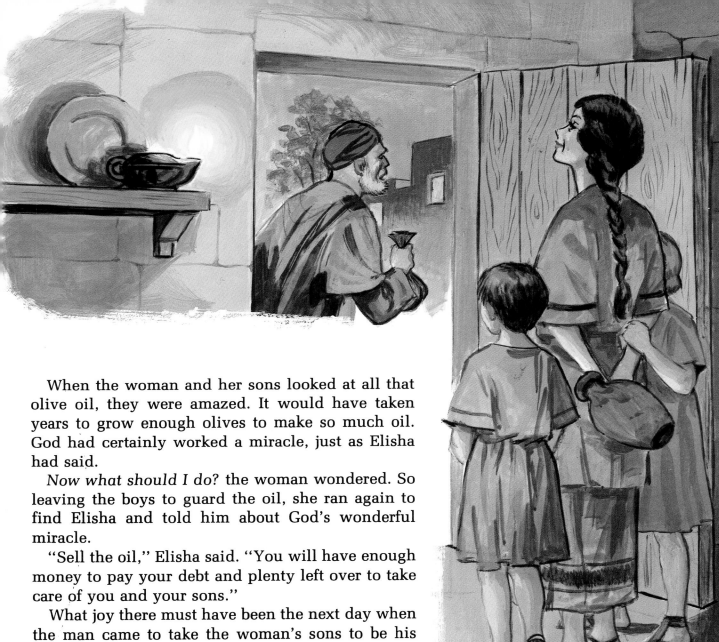

When the woman and her sons looked at all that olive oil, they were amazed. It would have taken years to grow enough olives to make so much oil. God had certainly worked a miracle, just as Elisha had said.

Now what should I do? the woman wondered. So leaving the boys to guard the oil, she ran again to find Elisha and told him about God's wonderful miracle.

"Sell the oil," Elisha said. "You will have enough money to pay your debt and plenty left over to take care of you and your sons."

What joy there must have been the next day when the man came to take the woman's sons to be his slaves! What a delight to hand the man his money! The debt was paid in full! God had worked a wonderful miracle, and their lives would always be different because of it.

WHAT DO YOU THINK?

1. Why do we call that a miracle? What did the woman need to do for the miracle to happen? What did the prophet do? What did God do?

2. Do you think God still does miracles today? Why do you think so? What does that story tell you that helps you believe in a miracle-working God?

The club started when Pookie wished he had a "millyun dollars." Maxi, Mini, Maria, and Big Bill thought it was a good idea, so they formed the Millionaires' Club.

Actually the sign said Millyun-air's Club. Pookie claimed credit for the sign until he heard it was misspelled. Then he blamed Maxi for it.

The five charter members chipped in to buy a can of gold-colored spray paint. Then they all helped spray a big pile of little rocks so they looked like gold nuggets.

"Now what do we do?" Pookie asked.

"First we have to divide the gold," said Big Bill. "Then we can buy things from each other. So let's each go home and get a container to hold the gold."

Maria was back first and waited at the club window. "A tin cup?" asked Pookie. But he filled it with gold.

Mini was next with an empty family-size peanut butter jar. Pookie shook his head and filled the jar with gold rocks.

"You don't think very big either," he mumbled.

Maxi thought a little bigger. He brought a two-pound coffee can and chuckled when he saw how much more gold he got than Maria or Mini. Then Pookie chuckled louder.

"Look behind you," said Pookie.

The Millyun-air's Club

There was Big Bill with a laundry pail in his hands. It held four times as much as Maxi's can. Pookie filled Big Bill's pail, but he was still smiling.

"Now what?" asked Maxi. "What's the big smile for?"

"This," said Pookie, bringing out a bushel basket from under the counter. Then Pookie filled his basket while the others frowned at him.

"Oink," said Maxi.

"Why oink me?" Pookie complained. "We agreed to bring a container for each of us. Some of us thought bigger than others. Let that be a lesson to you!"

"It's a good lesson," Poppi said that night when Maxi and Mini told him about the Millionaires' Club and the containers. "But the best lesson is something that Pookie may have missed."

"What was that, Poppi?" Maxi asked.

Then Poppi read the story about the miracle of the oil. "God gave this lady all that she could receive," said Poppi. "She received as much as her pots and jars would hold, no more. God would have given her twice as much oil, or ten times as much, if she had brought enough jars. That's the way it is with us, too. He wants to fill our big jars and baskets with His blessings, but we come to Him with our tin cups and peanut butter jars."

"Wow, I think I'll join another club," said Maxi.

"What's that?" asked Mini.

"God's millionaire club," said Maxi.

LET'S TALK ABOUT THIS

What this story teaches: God wants to give us more than we can receive. We are limited only by the size of the "vessel" we bring to Him.

1. How many blessings does God want to give you? Do you accept them by the cupful or the bushelful?
2. What did Maxi learn about receiving what God gives? What did you learn?

The Boy Who Lived Again

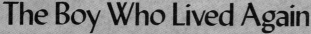

2 KINGS 4:18-37

For many years, a kind woman of Shunem had no children. For a woman of Israel that was a great shame. Every Israelite wanted children, especially a son.

Then one day Elisha promised the woman that God would work a miracle in her life. She would have a son.

Things happened exactly as Elisha said. The woman had a son at the very time Elisha said she would. She must have been the happiest woman in all the land.

The years passed, and the baby grew to be a strong boy. But one hot summer day when he was with his father and some reapers in the grainfields, the boy suddenly cried out.

"My head! My head!" he screamed.

The father and some nearby reapers ran over to the boy. By this time he had fallen to the ground.

"Carry him home to his mother," the father ordered.

Quickly one of the reapers gathered the boy into his arms and rushed toward the house. The mother tenderly took her son onto her lap and held him until noon, when he died.

At first the woman must have wondered what she should do. Where could she find help? Or was there any help now that her son had died? Then she remembered Elisha.

Quickly the woman carried her dead son to the room that she and her husband had built for Elisha. Trying to hide her tears, she ran to her husband and told him she wanted one of the servants and a donkey.

"I need to go to Elisha," she urged. "Hurry!"

The woman's husband was puzzled. "Why? It isn't the Sabbath or a new moon feast day," he said.

But the woman simply answered, "Everything will be all right." Then she saddled the donkey herself.

"Now go as fast as you can go!" the woman told the servant. "Don't slow down for me unless I tell you to." With that, the woman and her servant headed for Mount Carmel, where Elisha was staying.

Elisha saw the woman coming in the distance. "Here comes the woman from Shunem," he told his servant, Gehazi. "Go to meet her and ask if everything is all right with her and her family."

When Gehazi met her and asked if all was well, the woman kept on riding toward Elisha. "Everything is fine," she said, almost ignoring the servant.

As soon as the woman reached Elisha, she knelt down and clung to his feet. Gehazi tried to take her away, but Elisha would not let him.

"Let her alone," Elisha told his servant. "She has some great problem, and the Lord has not told me what it is." Then the woman told Elisha all that had happened.

"Take my staff and lay it on the child's face," Elisha told his servant. "Hurry!"

Elisha followed behind with the woman. But before they reached the woman's house, Gehazi came running toward them.

"Nothing has happened," Gehazi told them. "The child is still dead."

As soon as Elisha arrived at the woman's house, he shut the door behind him and pleaded with the Lord to help. Then he lay upon the boy's lifeless body, with his mouth, hands, and eyes close to the boy's mouth, hands, and eyes.

The boy became warm but still was not alive. So Elisha walked back and forth in the house, pleading again for the Lord to help. Then he returned to his room, where the boy lay on his bed, and stretched out upon him again.

With that, the boy sneezed seven times and was alive again.

"Tell the woman to come in now," Elisha told his servant.

Gehazi ran to get the woman. Of course she ran into the room as fast as she could. There was her son, alive and well again.

"Take your son in your arms," Elisha told her.

Elisha didn't need to say that. The woman threw her arms around her son and hugged him, as tears streamed down her face. Then she bowed down at Elisha's feet and thanked him again and again.

Elisha must have smiled as he watched the happy mother leave the room with her son. And perhaps he whispered a prayer something like this, "Thank You, Lord, for the miracle You have worked today."

WHAT DO YOU THINK?

1. How do you think the mother felt when her son died in her arms? How do you think she felt when her son was brought back to life?

2. Who really worked the miracle at Shunem, Elisha or God? What should we say to God when He does something for us?

37

The Princess Flower

Mini and Maxi thought it was such fun to help Mommi and Poppi plant tulip and daffodil bulbs in the fall. Poppi made the ground soft, until it felt good to touch. Mommi made a hole, and Maxi and Mini took turns popping in the bulbs and covering them with the rich soil.

"I can't wait to see all these beautiful flowers next spring," Mini said when the last bulb had been covered. "But how does God take an old bulb like this and bring a beautiful flower from it?"

Poppi smiled. "We don't know exactly how He does it," he said. "But He does it, just as He can bring people to life again. Which reminds me, I haven't told you the make-believe story of the Princess Flower, have I?"

Maxi and Mini clapped their hands. It was always fun to hear a Muffin make-believe story from Poppi. So the Muffins plopped down on the grass while Poppi told this story:

In a land far away there was a princess more beautiful than any other lady, near or far. She was so beautiful that the wind sighed by her castle each evening, and the sun smiled upon her each morning. Even the clouds of the sky wept for joy when they saw her, and their tears ran down her window.

The beautiful princess was not only beautiful to look at but was also beautiful in every other way. When the wind sighed, she laughed like the rippling of a brook and played tag with the wind.

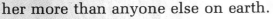

When the sun smiled upon her in the morning, the princess smiled back. That made the sun so happy that he ran across the sky all day until it was time to sleep at night.

The princess loved the beautiful clouds of the sky and often lay on a grassy hillside and played guessing games with them. The clouds became different shapes, and the princess guessed what they were.

That went on day after day. The sun, wind, and clouds became her dearest friends, and they loved her more than anyone else on earth.

But in a land not far away, an evil queen grew jealous of the beautiful princess. She wanted the sun to smile at her as he did at the princess. But whenever the sun looked at her evil face, he hid behind a cloud. She wanted the wind to sigh beside her castle, but whenever the wind came near it was so frightened that it raced away, creating great windstorms that blew dirt and sand into the sky by the queen's castle. The clouds felt so sorry for the queen and her evil ways that they often wept above her castle, mixing their tears in the great windstorms.

All of that made the queen even more jealous, for the land of the princess was bright and sunny and had soft winds and gentle showers. Her own land was filled with storms and cold gray skies.

One day the evil queen hid while the princess played games with the clouds. In the midst of the games she cast a spell upon the princess and turned her into a hard, strange, ugly lump. Now the beautiful princess looked like a tear drop, with brittle brown husks covering her. There were no smiles and no laughter, and the princess was no longer beautiful to see.

The wind, sun, and clouds buried their beautiful princess in the soft earth. The clouds watered her grave with their tears, and the wind sighed over it. The sun smiled each day, but it was so sad that it sank lower in the sky, which caused the land to grow cold and icy. The wind and clouds raced through the winter sky, angry and hurt.

40

But then one day the sun saw a beautiful green shoot coming from the princess's grave. He smiled a warm smile, which caused the green shoot to grow. The wind and clouds were happy, so they stopped their angry races, and they sent down warm tears of joy instead.

One morning the sun smiled his biggest smile. The clouds danced across the sky, and the winds sighed a gentle sigh. Then suddenly the green shoot burst open, and the beautiful princess stepped forth, wearing the most elegant purple robes that anyone had ever seen. She was more beautiful than ever, and the whole world smiled when it saw her.

Mini looked at the soft bed of tulips and daffodils. "Is that really the way it happened?" she asked.

Poppi smiled. "No, but it is a fun story you'll remember next spring when the tulips bloom, isn't it?"

"Right," said Mini, running toward a hillside nearby. "But I have to go now. I want to play some games with the clouds."

LET'S TALK ABOUT THIS

What this story teaches: God, who gave us life once, can give it to us a second time.

1. How does the growth of a tulip or daffodil from a bulb remind you of the boy who lived again? How does it remind you of Jesus, when He arose from the dead?

2. What does the word *resurrection* mean? What was the resurrection of Jesus? What does that mean for you some day?

Naaman's Greatest Victory

2 KINGS 5:1-15

Of all the soldiers of Syria, Naaman was the greatest. That is why the king of Syria made Naaman his general, in charge of all his soldiers.

During that time, Syria was mightier than Israel and often sent bands of soldiers into Israel to raid some of its cities. On one of those raids, some Syrian soldiers captured a little Israelite girl and General Naaman gave her to his wife to be a slave.

Naaman's wife was a kind lady and soon she and the girl loved each other as mother and daughter. But the girl noticed that Naaman's wife was often sad. One day she decided to ask her why.

"Naaman has leprosy," his wife told her.

Now the girl understood. If only there was something she could do to help her new mistress. Then she remembered Elisha, the prophet of God, back home in Israel. She decided to tell her mistress about him.

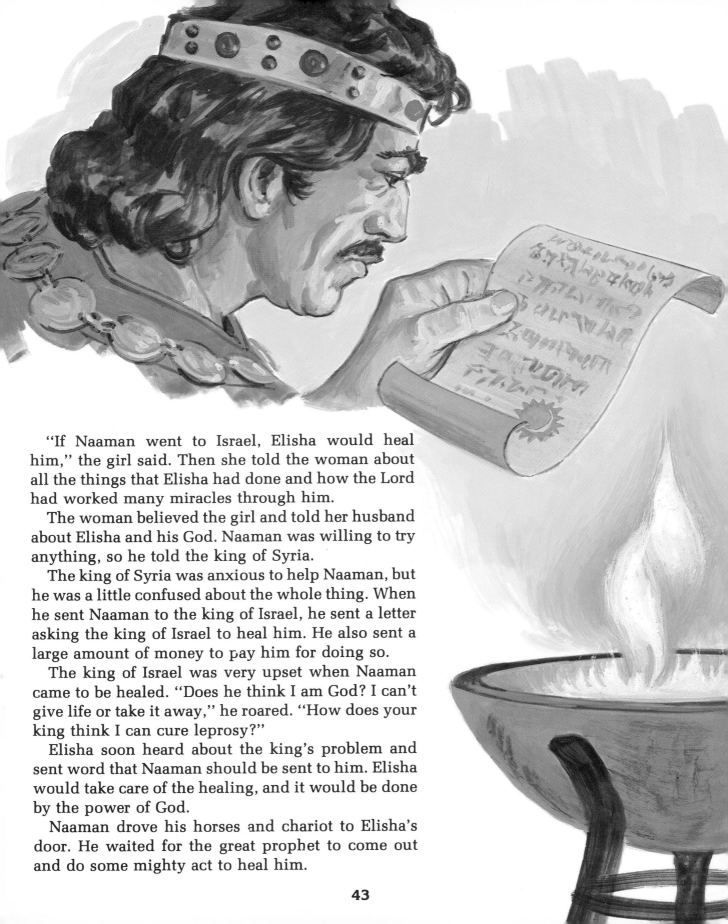

"If Naaman went to Israel, Elisha would heal him," the girl said. Then she told the woman about all the things that Elisha had done and how the Lord had worked many miracles through him.

The woman believed the girl and told her husband about Elisha and his God. Naaman was willing to try anything, so he told the king of Syria.

The king of Syria was anxious to help Naaman, but he was a little confused about the whole thing. When he sent Naaman to the king of Israel, he sent a letter asking the king of Israel to heal him. He also sent a large amount of money to pay him for doing so.

The king of Israel was very upset when Naaman came to be healed. "Does he think I am God? I can't give life or take it away," he roared. "How does your king think I can cure leprosy?"

Elisha soon heard about the king's problem and sent word that Naaman should be sent to him. Elisha would take care of the healing, and it would be done by the power of God.

Naaman drove his horses and chariot to Elisha's door. He waited for the great prophet to come out and do some mighty act to heal him.

Instead, Elisha sent his servant out to see Naaman. "You must go down to the Jordan River and wash in it seven times," the servant said. "Then your leprosy will be taken away."

Naaman was insulted, and very, very angry. The prophet had not even come outside his door to meet the great general from Syria. Instead, he had sent his servant. Not only that, he had told Naaman to wash in Israel's muddy Jordan River.

"Don't we have much better rivers in Syria?" Naaman shouted. "I thought that man would come out here and wave his hands over me and call upon his God to heal me."

With that, Naaman whirled his chariot around and headed for Syria as fast as he could go. But his servants caught up with him and talked with him.

"If the prophet had asked you to do something difficult, wouldn't you have done it?" they asked. "Instead, he has asked you to do something easy, like washing in the Jordan River. So why not do it?"

Naaman had calmed down by now. Perhaps the servants were right. Why not try?

Naaman turned his chariot around and headed for the Jordan River. When he arrived, he took off his clothes and went into the river. He went into the water once, but the white sores of his leprosy were still there. Down he went again, then again, and again. Six times he went into the Jordan River, and each time when he came out his white sores were still there. Then Naaman went down in the Jordan River once more, the seventh time. When he came out that time, all his white sores were gone. He was well again!

Naaman and his servants were so happy that they hardly knew what to do. Naaman dressed quickly, jumped into his chariot, and raced for Elisha's house.

Now Elisha was there to meet him. "I know that there is no other God in all the earth except your God," Naaman told Elisha.

Elisha was glad to hear Naaman say that. He knew it was true. But now Naaman, general of all the armies of Syria, knew also. That was Naaman's greatest victory.

WHAT DO YOU THINK?

1. Why couldn't Naaman help himself? Wasn't he one of the greatest men of his nation?

2. When Naaman went to ask Elisha for help, Elisha didn't even come out to see him but sent a servant to tell Naaman what to do. Why do you think Elisha did that? And why did he tell Naaman to wash in the Jordan River instead of a river in Syria?

3. What did Naaman learn about God? Why was that Naaman's greatest victory?

The Almost-wasn't Birthday

"Mini!"

"Yes, Mommi."

"Are you listening?"

"Yes, Mommi."

"I have to run uptown, Mini. Will you be my helper while I'm gone?"

"Yes, Mommi."

"At three o'clock, please turn off the oven and take out the cake. OK, Mini?"

"Yes, Mommi."

"Also, a deliveryman will come with some packages. The money for them is here on the counter. OK?"

"Yes, Mommi."

"One more thing. You must call Pookie, BoBo, Tony, and Maria and invite them to have cake and ice cream with you for your birthday tonight. Remember, Poppi and I said this morning that you could?"

"Yes, Mommi."

"Must be an interesting book, Mini. Please remember those three things. OK?"

"Yes, Mommi."

"Mini!"

"Yes, Mommi."

"I'm home now. Did you do what I asked?"

"Yes, Mommi."

"Mini! I smell something burning. Oh, Mini! Your birthday cake. It's burned to a crisp! Mini Muffin, come here! Didn't you remember to take this cake out?"

"No, Mommi. Did you ask me to?"

"Mini, I asked you and you heard me, but I don't think you were listening. Now what about the deliveryman?"

"A man came with some packages, but I didn't have the money to pay him, so he took them back."

"Your birthday gifts and the things for your party tonight. Now did you listen when I told you to invite your friends for this evening?"

"No, Mommi. I must have heard you, but I didn't listen."

"Well, it's 5:30—a little late in the day to invite friends to a little party without plates or napkins or gifts."

"Mini, happy birthday!"

"Oh, Poppi, am I glad to see you home. I really messed up my birthday. Mommi told me three things to do. I heard her but I wasn't listening."

"I'm sorry, Mini. Now would you like to take these packages to Mommi. I met the deliveryman down the street. He said he couldn't deliver these here and maybe I'd like to take them home."

"My birthday gifts! The things for my party! I'm listening. Oh, Mommi, here they are!"

"And here is a box of blueberry muffins. I just couldn't resist when I saw them at the bakery."

"Oh, Poppi, those will be my birthday cake! I'll put a candle on each one. Oh, if only my friends were here!"

"Well, the doorbell is ringing. Why don't you see who it is?"

"Happy birthday, Mini!"

"Maria!"

"And Pookie, BoBo, Tony, and Maxi are behind me. Maxi said you'd forget to invite us, so he did. Mini, did you hear me?"

"Oh, Maria, I didn't just hear you. I'M LISTEN-ING!"

LET'S TALK ABOUT THIS

What this story teaches: God—and parents—can do wonderful things for us when we listen to instructions.

1. How did Mini almost miss her birthday things? Did she hear? Did she listen? What is the difference?

2. Do you sometimes hear your parents but do not listen to what they say? Do you sometimes hear what your Bible says but do not really listen to it? What should you do?

STORIES JESUS TOLD

The Lost Sheep
LUKE 15:1-7

The Pharisees and scribes of Israel always found something to grumble about. They did not like Jesus because He told the people to obey God's laws. They expected the people to obey their laws too.

So they watched Jesus, hoping that He would do something wrong. Then they could complain about Him.

One day the Pharisees and scribes watched the people who came to hear Jesus. They saw tax collectors in the crowd. Everyone knew that tax collectors cheated their own people and collected taxes for the Romans. They also saw people who were known for their sins.

"Do you see what kind of people come to hear Him?" the Pharisees and scribes asked each other. "Jesus even welcomes them and eats with them."

Jesus knew what those people were saying about Him. So He told them a story.

"Suppose one of you had a hundred sheep and one should become lost," Jesus began. "Would you not leave the ninety-nine safe in the sheepfold and go out into the desert to look for that one lost sheep?"

Some of the Pharisees and scribes began to nod their heads. They knew that was true, for many of them owned sheep, and they certainly would go out to look for one that was lost. They knew that any shepherd would search for days to find that one lost sheep.

"When a shepherd finds a lost sheep, he is filled with joy," Jesus continued. "He puts it on his shoulders and takes it home. The shepherd is so happy to have his lost sheep back that he calls in his friends and neighbors and asks them to rejoice with him."

The Pharisees and scribes listened carefully. They knew exactly how a shepherd felt when he found a lost sheep. And they would feel the same way.

"In the same way, there is joy in heaven when one sinner repents," Jesus went on. "There will be greater joy for that one sinner than for ninety-nine good people."

As far as we know, the Pharisees and scribes said nothing more at that time. Perhaps they were ashamed. They of all people should have rejoiced when a sinner came to God to ask forgiveness. Instead, they grumbled about it. If they complained and heaven rejoiced, perhaps the Pharisees and scribes were out of tune with heaven! And who could tell them more about heaven than Jesus, for heaven was His home?

WHAT DO YOU THINK?

1. Why were the scribes and Pharisees complaining? What would you have said to them when they complained?

2. Jesus told them a story about a lost sheep. What kind of people are like that lost sheep? What happened when the lost sheep was found? What happens when a lost person repents, or feels sorry for his sins, and comes to God? Have you asked God to forgive your sins? If not, would you like to now?

A Ruff Night

"It will be dark when we get to Thatcher's Woods," Poppi told Maxi and Mini. "Do you mind?"

"Not if we can find Ruff," Maxi answered.

"We must find him," Mini moaned. "Why did he run after those squirrels like that this afternoon when Maxi and I were there with him? Oh, Poppi, we will find him, won't we?"

"I'm sure we will, Mini," said Poppi. "He probably crossed the stream and then lost his scent coming back. Now let's get some flashlights and be on our way."

It was dark when the Muffins reached Thatcher's Woods. There was no moon in the sky, so the trees seemed large and spooky to Mini, not at all the friendly trees she and Maxi had played under that afternoon.

"Can you find your way back?" Mini asked Poppi.

"Poppi and I have hiked here many years," Mommi said. "I'm sure Poppi could find his way without the flashlights."

Mini and Maxi didn't like that idea. But they did like Poppi's idea to stay together.

Again and again the Muffins called Ruff's name. They went down the path and crossed the stream, then followed the path on the other side. Each time after they called, the Muffins stopped for several moments in silence to listen for Ruff to answer.

The Muffins called and listened for what seemed like hours. At last Mini plopped onto an old log by the path and began to cry.

"He's gone! I know it!" she sobbed.

Poppi looked at his watch. "Look, we've been out here two hours already. Do you want to give up and go home?"

"OH, NO!" Maxi cried out. "We can't leave Ruff out here alone. We'll go on all night if we must."

"Then maybe we should do what we should have done when we left home," Mommi suggested. "We forgot to pray."

"You're right," said Poppi. "If we are going out to seek and to find the lost, we'd better ask the Good Shepherd to guide us."

So the Muffins each prayed that their Good Shepherd would help them find their lost Ruff. Then they were on their way again, calling and listening, listening and calling.

"Let's sing!" said Mommi. "Ruff can hear that as well as shouting. Besides, it will cheer us up."

The Muffins sat on a big log and began to sing. They sang songs about Jesus. They even sang one song about the Shepherd who went out to look for one lost sheep, leaving ninety-nine safe in the fold.

Suddenly the Muffins heard a rustling in the leaves along the trail. Then they heard a yipping and whining. Four flashlights turned toward the trail and focused on a very excited, happy bundle of fur.

"RUFF!" Mini cried out.

"We have found you!" shouted Maxi.

"The lost sheep has been found," said Poppi. "So let's take him home where we can rejoice together."

Maxi squeezed Ruff into his arms. Poppi swooped Mini into his. And Mommi tried to guide them back with four flashlights in her hands.

"This is certainly a Ruff night," she said. Everyone had a good laugh about that—except Ruff, who was fast asleep in Maxi's arms.

LET'S TALK ABOUT THIS

What this story teaches: Good friends and good family, like the Good Shepherd, search for the lost ones they love until they find them.

1. Why did the Muffins search until they found Ruff? Why not just leave him in the woods until morning and then look for him?

2. What do you think they talked about on the way home? What does it mean when someone says a person is lost, away from God? How can we help that person come to God through Jesus?

The Lost Coin

LUKE 15:8-10

When some Pharisees and scribes complained that Jesus welcomed tax collectors and sinful people to listen to His teaching, Jesus told them a story about a lost sheep. "Any good shepherd will leave ninety-nine sheep safe in the sheepfold and go out to look for one that is lost," Jesus told them. "When he returns with the lost sheep, his friends and neighbors rejoice with him. In the same way, heaven rejoices when one lost sinner turns from his sins and comes to God."

Jesus then told the Pharisees and scribes another story, somewhat like the one about the lost sheep. That one was about a lost coin.

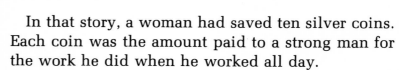

In that story, a woman had saved ten silver coins. Each coin was the amount paid to a strong man for the work he did when he worked all day.

The woman kept her ten silver coins in a jar hidden in her home. She liked to take the jar from its hiding place and look at the coins. It was hard for anyone to save money in Bible times. It was especially hard for a poor woman to save so much.

But one day when she took the jar down and began to count her coins, the woman grew frightened. She counted, then counted again. But each time she counted only nine coins.

"How terrible," she must have cried out. "I had ten coins. One of them is lost."

The woman ran to find a lamp. That was something like a covered gravy dish with a wick in one end. It was filled with olive oil.

The woman lit her lamp. She looked in every corner of the room. But she could not find her lost coin.

Next the woman ran to get her broom. She swept every part of that room until the broom sent something spinning across the floor.

It was the lost coin! The woman bent down with her lamp, and there in a dark corner was the precious coin. The lost had been found.

Like the shepherd who found his lost sheep, the woman rejoiced because she had found her lost coin. And, like the shepherd, she had to share the news with her friends and neighbors. Because they were good friends and neighbors, they rejoiced with her.

When Jesus finished telling that story, He spoke to the Pharisees, scribes, and others standing nearby.

"The angels of God rejoice whenever a sinner repents, turns from his sin, and comes to God," He said. "It is just like the rejoicing of the shepherd and his friends over the lost sheep. And it is like the rejoicing of the woman and her friends over the lost coin."

People who have never come to God through Jesus are lost. God calls them that for they are not safe in God's loving care. But there is great joy in heaven when one person turns away from sin and asks Jesus to lead him or her to God.

WHAT DO YOU THINK?

1. Have you ever heard people talk of someone who was lost? What did they mean? Have you heard of people "repenting" or "being saved"? What does that mean?

2. Repenting means to be sorry for the sins in our lives and to turn from them. To be saved means to ask Jesus to take away our sin and give us a new life in God. When we do that, even the angels in heaven rejoice.

A CHARM-ing Party

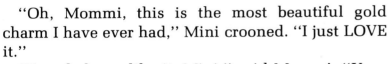

"Oh, Mommi, this is the most beautiful gold charm I have ever had," Mini crooned. "I just LOVE it."

"I'm glad you like it, Mini," said Mommi. "Your grandmommi gave it to me when I was a girl your age. I decided that you're old enough to have it."

"But it's so tiny," said Mini.

"Yes, as soon as Poppi comes home, we'll ask him to put it on your charm bracelet," Mommi added. "Until then be careful. It would be easy to lose."

"Oh, I won't lose it," said Mini. "I'll hold it tight all day."

Mini did hold it tight. That is, until she realized that she wasn't holding it tight.

"But I had it right here in my hand," Mini whispered to herself. "Where did it go?"

Mini looked at the sofa where she had been sitting. It could have fallen between the cushions. But then she did walk to her room, so there was a long stretch of rug where it could have fallen. It could be anywhere.

"I must run downtown to do some chores, Mini," Mommi called from the kitchen. "I'll be back in a couple of hours."

"OK, Mommi," Mini answered.

When Mini heard the door slam, she took all the cushions from the sofa and ran her hand along the back. "Two hours," she whispered. "I must find this charm before Mommi comes home. What will I tell her if I don't?"

Mini was sure she had covered every inch of that sofa. Then she put the cushions on again.

Next she got on her hands and knees and began to feel in the rug for her charm. She spread the rug apart as she crawled along, looking in every place she thought she had walked on the way to her room. Mini was sure she had covered every tiny piece of the rug between the sofa and her room. She was sure also that it must be almost time for Mommi to come home.

By the time Mini reached her room, the tears were streaming down her cheeks. She looked through the fibers of the rug in her room. Then she opened her jewelry box to make sure she hadn't put it there by mistake.

Mini was sobbing by now as she looked in her dresser drawers and on her desk. She even looked in all the pockets of the clothes in the closet.

Mommi would be home any minute now. Mini was frantic. She could NOT find her beautiful charm.

Sobbing as if she had lost her best friend, Mini plopped onto her bed. What would she tell Mommi? But just as she wondered that, her hand touched something hard and small. Mini looked down toward her hand.

"MY CHARM!" she shouted, almost screaming. "MY CHARM! MY CHARM! MY CHARM! I found it!"

Just then the door closed, and Mimi ran toward the sound of the door as fast as she could go, clutching her charm tight in her hand. She was running so fast that she almost knocked Poppi and Mommi over.

"I FOUND IT! I FOUND IT!" Mini shouted.

"Hmmm, let me guess," said Poppi. "A million dollars? No, wait. It's got to be at least two million."

"Oh, Poppi, no, more than that," said Mini.

"THREE million!" said Poppi. "I won't go any higher than that."

Mini giggled. "I lost the beautiful charm Mommi gave me." She sighed. "And I've been looking for it ever since Mommi left two hours ago."

"I'm so glad you found it, Mini," said Mommi. "Now perhaps Poppi will put it on your charm bracelet."

"Oh, Mommi, please let me ask some of my friends over for some ice cream," Mini begged. "I'm just so happy I found it that I want to tell my friends."

Mommi smiled. "Sounds like the story of the lost coin we read a couple of nights ago," she said. "Yes, you may rejoice with your friends."

"Sounds like a CHARM-ing party to me." Poppi chuckled as he went to get his tools.

LET'S TALK ABOUT THIS

What this story teaches: When the lost is found, it brings great joy. That is especially true when a lost person comes to Jesus.

1. Why was Mini so happy when she found her lost charm? Were you happy with her? Do you think her friends will be happy with her, too?
2. Why are Christian friends happy when someone they love accepts Jesus as Savior? How is that like finding a lost coin or a lost charm?
3. Have you accepted Him as your Savior? Would that make someone happy if you did? Who?

THREE WOMEN WHO MET JESUS

The Woman at the Well
JOHN 4:4-42

The great Passover feast had ended. As usual, it had been a time of great excitement, when families and friends gathered in Jerusalem to talk, to eat together, and to worship together in the Temple. Each year, during the Passover, the people did almost the same things that they had done for many years at the Passover feast.

But some things were different that time. For example, Jesus had surprised His disciples one day by picking up a whip and driving merchants and money changers from the Temple. He had angrily told them that the Temple was God's house, a place for worship, and not a den of thieves.

The disciples had also been surprised one night when a member of the council came to ask Jesus about heaven. Most of the council members did not like Jesus. Some even wanted to kill Him. But that man listened carefully while Jesus told him how he could accept new life from God through His Son and be born again.

Now, on their way home, the disciples must have talked much about those things. They were still talking about them when Jesus led them into Samaria.

Most of the people of Israel would not travel through Samaria. They went many miles out of their way to go around the region. They hated the Samaritans, for they were a "mixed people," whose ancestors were both Jews and foreigners.

Of course Jesus did not hate the Samaritans or any other people. He had come to earth to teach and to die for all people, including the Samaritans.

Jesus stopped for lunch at an old well near the village of Sychar. While the disciples went into town to buy food, Jesus waited at the well. Before long, a Samaritan woman came to the well to get water.

"Please give Me a drink of water," Jesus said to the woman.

The woman was surprised. "You are a Jew, and You ask a Samaritan woman for some water?" she asked.

"Yes, but you should have asked Me for water instead," Jesus answered. "I have the kind of water that will take away your thirst forever."

"That would be wonderful," the woman said. "Then I would never have to come to this well again."

The woman did not understand that Jesus was talking about giving her new life that would satisfy her forever. Jesus knew that He must help her understand Who He was.

"Why not bring your husband here?" Jesus suggested.

"I have no husband," the woman answered.

"I know," said Jesus. Then He told her things about herself that no ordinary man would know. The woman was amazed that Jesus could do that.

"You are a prophet!" she said. Then she asked Jesus to tell her about God and how people should worship Him.

"When the Messiah, God's Son, comes He will know about such things," the woman said.

"He has come!" said Jesus. "You are talking with Him now."

Just then the disciples returned with the food for lunch. They were surprised that Jesus was talking with a Samaritan woman, but said nothing.

While the disciples prepared lunch, the woman ran back to Sychar to tell her friends and neighbors about Jesus. She wanted to share the good news with them.

"Please eat," the disciples told Jesus when lunch was ready.

"Thank you, but I do not need to eat now," Jesus answered. "I have other kinds of food."

Jesus pointed to the gates of Sychar, where the woman's friends and neighbors were streaming out to listen to Him.

"Some people say the time of harvest is four months away," Jesus said. "But I say it is now." Jesus was speaking, of course, about the many people who would come to know Him personally and believe in Him as God's Son. That was a harvest of people for God's Kingdom.

Jesus and His disciples stayed at Sychar two days. Many Samaritans believed what Jesus said and accepted Him as Savior. The disciples realized now that Jesus truly gave "living water" to those people, for as they accepted Him, and believed in Him, He satisfied them in a way that would last forever.

WHAT DO YOU THINK?

1. Where did the Samaritan woman go when she was thirsty? Did the water from the well help her?
2. Why did Jesus say that people who accepted Him would never thirst again?
3. Have you accepted Jesus into your heart? Would you like to now?

The King's Highway

"I need a wise ambassador to take my good news to the people," the king announced one day. "Who will do this for me?"

Three knights came to the castle, each hoping to be chosen for that work. They were Sir Yessir, Sir Forgetyousir, and Sir Smarterthanyousir.

"Whoever delivers this message first to the far side of my kingdom shall be my ambassador," said the king. Then the king gave each a message.

"The King's Highway will take you there fastest," said the king. "Do not be deceived when other roads seem better."

"That's all I need to know," said Sir Smarterthanyousir. Off he went with the royal message. He thought he was smarter than the king and would get a head start on the other two knights.

"If you linger with me for a time, I will show you a fountain with the Water of Life," said the king. "Fill your canteens with that, and you will never thirst on the highway."

Forget you, sir! Sir Forgetyousir thought to himself. *You're trying to delay me.* So he started on the King's Highway. He would not listen to the king's commands. He would not follow what the king said. He would do things his own way.

But Sir Yessir lingered behind. "I will follow your commands exactly," he said. "Whatever you say, I will do it, for you are wiser than all the knights of the land, and you want what is best for your ambassador."

Sir Yessir filled his canteen with the Water of Life. He talked with the king and came to know him personally. He knew that he could trust the king completely. Then he started out on the King's Highway.

The sun grew hotter and hotter as the morning went by. At almost high noon, Sir Yessir heard someone calling him. It was Sir Smarterthanyousir.

"Come on this road with me," he called. "It is much better than the King's Highway. I'm smarter than the king, as you can see."

"No," said Sir Yessir. "The road only appears to be better. I will stay on the King's Highway."

"Foolish man," said Sir Smarterthanyousir. Then off he went, and no one heard from him again.

Sir Yessir kept on going through the heat of the day. Often he stopped to drink of the Water of Life. About midafternoon he heard another voice calling. It was Sir Forgetyousir. He was sitting in the shade of a big tree beside the highway.

"Still following the king's orders?" asked Sir Forgetyousir. "I gave that up in the heat of the day. It's much more comfortable to sit in the shade of this tree than to go running across the kingdom."

Sir Yessir kept going on the King's Highway. The Water of Life had satisfied his thirst all along the way. He would follow the king exactly.

At last, toward evening, Sir Yessir saw a man standing in the highway ahead.

"This is the other side of the kingdom," said the man. "You have reached it because you followed my commands. Now you shall be my ambassador."

Sir Yessir looked more closely. The man in the road was the king.

LET'S TALK ABOUT THIS

What this story teaches: Believing in Jesus and following Him satisfies us as water satisfies thirsty people.

1. How does the Water of Life that the king gave remind you of the living water in the Bible story?
2. Why did Sir Yessir reach his goal when the other two did not? What did you learn from this?

Who Touched My Clothes?

MARK 5:21-34

"Help me!"

"Heal me!"

"Teach me!"

Everywhere Jesus went, crowds of people went with him. They cried out for help. They asked Him to heal them. And they begged Him to tell them more about God and His heavenly home.

One day Jesus and His disciples sailed home from the other side of the Sea of Galilee. As usual, crowds from Capernaum gathered around His boat as He came to shore.

The people pressed toward Jesus as He stepped upon the beach. Each wanted to get closer than his neighbor. As Jesus walked from the shore, the people moved even closer to Him. Each one wanted to ask Him to help, or heal, or teach something. Jesus looked about the crowd. There were so many who needed help.

Suddenly Jesus stopped. He looked from person to person.

"Who touched My clothes?" He asked.

The disciples were surprised. "What do You mean?" they asked. "Don't You see all these people pressing against You? Why do You ask who touched Your clothes?"

But Jesus still looked at the people around Him. He knew that someone had touched His clothes, for the power to heal had flowed from Him.

Suddenly the crowd grew quiet. A woman had fallen on her knees before Jesus, trembling and frightened. Then she told Jesus her story.

For twelve years she had suffered with a sore that would not stop bleeding. She had spent all her money, going from doctor to doctor, trying to be healed. But no one could help her. Instead, she got worse.

Then the woman heard that Jesus was passing by. *If only I can touch the fringe at the bottom of His cloak, I will get well,* she thought.

The woman believed that so much that she moved through the crowd to get to Jesus. In a moment of great faith, she reached out and touched His clothes. At that moment, she was healed.

Jesus must have smiled at that woman who had shown such great faith in Him. "Your faith has cured you," Jesus told her. "Go in peace, for your sickness has left you. You are well!"

The woman was too happy to speak. But as Jesus turned to go, her heart must have sung with joy. She was well! The years of suffering and sickness were over. Her life was new again, all because of Jesus.

WHAT DO YOU THINK?

1. How would you feel if you had been sick for twelve years and no doctor could help you? What would you want Jesus to do for you?

2. If you were sick and Jesus came to your town, would you try to touch His clothes to be healed? How would you feel if suddenly you were well? What would you think about Jesus?

King Maxi Midas

"Why such a cheerful face, Maxi?"

"Don't be cute, Mini. I'm so broke I can't even buy a chocolate sundae."

Maxi looked like Mr. Gloom himself as he sat on the old stump, with his chin in his hands.

"Remember the story about King Midas and his golden touch?" Maxi added. "Wow! Wouldn't that be fun for one day to turn things to gold by touching them?"

"Well, your friends and family would certainly stay away from you," said Mini.

Maxi was still thinking about King Midas and the golden touch when he went to bed that night. Maxi set his alarm for the next morning.

"KA-ZOOM!" he said as he touched the clock. "See, if I had the golden touch, that clock would turn to pure gold."

Then Maxi reached up to turn off his lamp. "KA-ZAM," he said. "A golden lamp. Wow! That would buy ten thousand chocolate sundaes."

Before long, Maxi had drifted off to sleep. He dreamed that he was King Maxi Midas and that he really did have the golden touch.

"KA-ZOOM!" Some flowers turned to gold.

"KA-ZAM!" Trees and bushes became pure gold, gleaming in the sunlight.

"Wonder how many chocolate sundaes that golden tree would buy?" Maxi chuckled.

Maxi was so busy KA-ZAM-ing and KA-ZOOM-ing that he didn't hear Mini ride up on her beautiful horse.

"What's going on?" Mini asked.

"We're rich!" said King Maxi Midas. "Let's go down to Pop's Sweet Shop in the village, and I'll buy you a chocolate sundae as big as a house."

"Oh, that's wonderful!" said Mini. "Jump on my horse with me, and we'll go right now."

But as soon as King Maxi Midas jumped on the horse with Mini—KA-ZAM!—both Mini and her horse turned into a golden statue.

"OH, NO!" shouted the king. "Mini has turned to gold. What will I do?"

The king forgot about turning things to gold and ran for the palace as fast as he could go.

"Mommi! Poppi!" he cried out as he ran. But as he ran through the palace, he left behind a trail of golden doorknobs, golden carpets, and golden statues of bowing guards.

At last he found Mommi and Poppi sitting in the palace living room, reading the royal newspaper.

"Mommi! Poppi! Something terrible has happened to Mini," King Maxi Midas shouted. Then he threw his arms around them. KA-ZOOM! KA-ZAM! There was a golden statue of Mommi and a golden statue of Poppi.

Before Maxi could say anything, he felt the royal dog and royal cat rubbing against him. But they didn't rub very long before they turned into a golden Ruff and a golden Tuff.

"MOMMI! POPPI! MINI! RUFF! TUFF!" King Maxi Midas shouted over and over again.

Then King Maxi felt a warm tender touch on his hand. "Don't touch me!" he shouted. "You'll turn to gold."

"I hope not," Mommi's soft voice answered. "Then who would wake you up when you have bad dreams?"

Maxi's eyes fluttered open. There was Mommi, with her hand on his. And there was Poppi, and Mini, and Ruff and Tuff, all standing beside his bed.

"Oh, my wonderful family!" said Maxi. "You're worth more to me than all the gold in the world."

"That's a lot of chocolate sundaes," said Poppi, chuckling. "Are we REALLY worth that much?"

"MUCH more!" said Maxi. "MUCH, MUCH more."

LET'S TALK ABOUT THIS

What this story teaches: The warm personal touch of those we love is much more important than all the money in the world. As the woman touched Jesus, she discovered that He touched her life to change it.

1. Have you, like Maxi, ever wished for all the money in the world? What would you do with it?

2. What did Maxi learn was worth more—his family or all the gold in the world? Would you give up your family for a million dollars? Would you give up Jesus for a million dollars? Why not?

Faith in a Foreign Land
MATTHEW 15:21-28; MARK 7:24-30

"Why are we leaving Israel?" some of Jesus' disciples asked. The others shook their heads. They did not know either.

The disciples had wondered about that when Jesus left Galilee with them and headed north toward Tyre and Sidon. Why there? Why leave their own land where crowds waited hungrily for Jesus to heal them and teach them about God?

Jesus had told the disciples to keep their trip a secret. That, too, seemed strange to them. Why? What was He planning to do?

The disciples were still wondering about those things when they reached the area near Tyre and Sidon. Suddenly a woman from that area ran toward them and fell on her knees before Jesus.

"Have mercy on me," she begged. "My daughter has a demon in her. Please make it go out of her, and heal her."

At first Jesus pretended not to hear her. He waited to see what the disciples would say.

The disciples did not like that woman to ask Jesus for help. She was a Canaanite woman, a foreigner whose people did not believe in God. How dare she ask Jesus for anything!

Of course the disciples did not know that Jesus had come on that long trip to meet the foreign woman. And how could they know that she would help them learn something very important about Jesus?

"Send her away," the disciples told Jesus. "She is bothering us with her begging."

Jesus must have looked with pity at His disciples. Because the poor woman was a foreigner, they did not want her daughter to be freed from a demon. If she had been an Israelite, they would have asked Jesus to heal her.

Jesus was not quite ready yet to show the disciples why He had come to meet the woman. First He must test the woman's faith. He must let the disciples hear for themselves how she believed in Him.

"Don't you realize that I have been sent to the people of Israel?" Jesus asked the woman. "Is it right to take what is theirs and give it to people who are like dogs?"

The woman knew exactly what Jesus meant. Most of her friends and neighbors around Tyre and Sidon had no more faith in God than a dog would have. So instead of arguing that she was different from her neighbors, the woman humbly told Jesus how she trusted Him for His help.

"Lord, remember that dogs are willing to eat crumbs from their master's table," she said.

Jesus looked at His disciples. Surely they could see by now that the woman trusted in Him as much as any Israelite did. Now they must learn that He would not turn away any needy person who came to Him, trusting Him for help.

"Great is your faith," Jesus told the woman. "You shall have what you asked Me to give."

A woman of little faith might have asked Jesus to prove that her daughter back home was healed. Or perhaps she would have asked Jesus to go back home with her just to be sure the healing had worked.

But that woman believed so much in Jesus that she knew her daughter was healed. She thanked Jesus for healing her and rushed home to find her daughter well again.

While all of that happened, the disciples stood by, very much surprised. Their eyes had seen and their ears had heard that foreign woman who had such great faith in Jesus. Was there anyone back in Galilee who had shown a greater faith in Him?

Now the disciples knew why Jesus had brought them here. They must have been ashamed that they had wanted to send the woman away without help when she had shown such great faith in Jesus.

As the disciples followed Jesus back to Galilee, they must have thought much about the Canaanite woman who believed in Jesus. Surely they must have realized now that Jesus had come to seek and to save any lost person, no matter who he was or where he lived.

WHAT DO YOU THINK?

1. What kind of woman was in the story? Why did the disciples want Jesus to send her away?
2. Why didn't Jesus help the woman as soon as she came to see Him?
3. What did the disciples learn about Jesus? What did you learn about Him?

My Friend Maxi

"Tony, you're my friend, aren't you?"

"Sure, Pookie, what do you need?"

Pookie hung his head. "Well, I accidentally broke Mr. Crabberry's window with my ball," he said. "I want to tell him that I did it and that I will work to pay for it. Will you go with me to tell him?"

"Sorry, Pookie," said Tony. "But old Mr. Crabberry will think I did it too. I don't want to work for your window."

"I don't want you to work for it," said Pookie. "I just need a friend when I go to tell him."

But before Pookie could say anything further, Tony was gone. Just then Big Bill came along.

"Eating lemons today?" asked Big Bill.

"I just need a friend," said Pookie. "Will you be a pal for me?"

"Sure, Pookie," said Bill. "Anything! Just tell me what you need."

But before Pookie could finish telling Bill about Mr. Crabberry's window, Bill was hurrying "for a very important appointment."

BoBo was next. He didn't even volunteer to be a friend. BoBo was suspicious from the very beginning. "Sorry, Pookie, can't help you," BoBo said as soon as he saw that Pookie needed something.

"Fine bunch of friends they are," Pookie grumbled as he sat in the shade of a big tree. "Just because I'm in trouble, no one wants to be a friend."

"I do," said a voice.

Pookie looked up.

"Maxi!" he said. "I didn't hear you come up."

"I was just watching to see if you would cave in," said Maxi. "Why do you need a friend right now?"

"Mr. Crabberry," said Pookie.

"You DO need a friend," said Maxi.

"I broke his window," Pookie added.

"Wow! You REALLY need a friend," said Maxi.

"And I want to tell Mr. Crabberry and let him know that I will pay for it and have it put in," said Pookie. "But I'm afraid to go alone. I need a friend to go with me."

Maxi whistled. "You need a SPECIAL friend," he said. "Do you want your special friend strung up by the thumbs with you?"

Pookie didn't think that was very funny. "It isn't that bad, is it, Maxi?" he asked. "But that's OK. I understand why you won't go with me."

"That's not what I said," Maxi answered. "I'm ready when you are."

"You mean you will go with me?" asked Pookie. "Really?"

Maxi almost had to push Pookie up to Mr. Crabberry's front door. He even rang the doorbell for him. Then when Mr. Crabberry opened the door, Pookie stammered and stuttered until Mr. Crabberry told him to speak up.

"What he means, sir, is that he broke your window and wants to work for you to pay for it," Maxi chimed in.

"Izzatso?" said Mr. Crabberry. "Well, now, it's nice to know that I have honest neighbors. But I'm afraid you'd better work for your father instead of me."

"Wh . . . why?" asked Pookie.

"Because your ball didn't break my window," Mr. Crabberry replied. "It hit my house and bounced back into your window."

"MY window?" Pookie gasped. "MAXI, LOOK! It really is MY window, the window to MY room. Thanks, Mr. Crabberry, for understanding."

Before long, Pookie and Maxi had cleaned up all the glass and mess in Pookie's room. "My poppi said he would help me put the glass in this afternoon," said Pookie. "I'll go get it now at the hardware store. Thanks, Maxi, for being not only a friend, but a REAL friend and a SPECIAL friend."

"That's OK, Pookie," said Maxi. "Next time I bounce a ball into my own window, I'll call on you for help."

LET'S TALK ABOUT THIS

What this story teaches: Maxi would not turn from someone who needed him, just as Jesus would not turn from the woman who needed Him.

1. What kind of friends were Bill, Tony, and BoBo? What kind of friend was Maxi?
2. What should a person do when a friend needs him or her? What did Jesus do when the woman needed Him? What did Maxi do when Pookie needed him?
3. What kind of friend are you? What do you do for Jesus when He needs you?

PAUL-MISSIONARY WITH POWER

The Burning Books

ACTS 19:11-20

From city to city Paul went throughout the ancient world, telling people about Jesus. He told them how Jesus, God's Son, had come to earth and how He had died upon the cross.

Some believed in Jesus as God's Son, but many turned away, refusing to believe. Then Paul taught the new believers how to live for Jesus and how to tell others about Him.

The city of Ephesus was a great city where important people from all over the ancient world came to trade with each other. It was also a city that had a large, beautiful temple built to honor Diana, a goddess in whom many of those people believed.

Paul visited the synagogue when he came to Ephesus and tried to tell his own Jewish people about Jesus. But after three months, Paul saw that many of his people were growing farther from Jesus and not closer to Him. So Paul moved his little church over to a school building and preached there for about two years.

During that time, many sick people came to Paul and he healed them. Sometimes people could not bring a sick person to Paul, so they carried away a towel or handkerchief that Paul had touched, and when the sick person also touched it, he was healed.

84

Many people were impressed that Paul could drive demons from people, and some thought secret magic must be in the words "in Jesus' name." So they tried to drive out demons also.

Among those who tried were seven sons of the Jewish high priest Sceva. One day they saw a man who had a demon in him. They followed him to his home, for they were anxious to try their "new magic" on the man.

As soon as they could get near the man, they recited the words "Come out of that man, in Jesus' name."

The demon in the man was amused. "Well, I know Jesus, and I know Paul," it said. "But who do you think you are?"

With that, the demon caused the man to jump on those seven sons and give them a beating they would never forget. Of course, the news spread all over Ephesus, and many began to respect the name of Jesus more, some believing in Jesus and accepting Him as God's Son and their Savior.

Among those who became Christians were many who had practiced magic, using certain books that were written for that purpose. When they accepted Jesus as Savior, they brought those evil books to Paul and confessed their sins, turning away from all those things.

When a great pile of those evil books of magic had been brought, the people burned them. That was not done in secret but in a public place, where all the people of Ephesus would know what they had done.

Great and mighty things continued to happen at Ephesus as Paul preached about the Lord Jesus. Many believed, and the power of the Lord spread through their lives.

WHAT DO YOU THINK?

1. Why could Paul drive out demons when other people failed?

2. What caused all those great and mighty things to happen in Ephesus? What happened in the lives of the people who accepted Jesus as God's Son and Savior?

The Bible Club

"Pookie! Are you coming to Bible club with me tonight?"

"Maxi! Shhhhhhh! Do you have to say those things while my friends are listening?"

Maxi looked puzzled. "Don't your friends like Bible clubs?" he asked.

Pookie frowned. "I don't know, but you just don't run around school shouting about Bible clubs, that's all."

Maxi shrugged his shoulders. He wasn't sure what Pookie meant, but he didn't want to bug him now.

A moment later Maxi saw BoBo at the other end of the hallway. "BoBo," he called. "Wait up!"

BoBo and a couple of his friends stopped to wait for Maxi.

"Are you coming to Bible club with me tonight, BoBo?" Maxi asked.

BoBo turned a light shade of pink. "Sorry, I can't talk with you now," BoBo stammered. "The fellas and I have to go, don't we?"

With that, BoBo hurried down the hallway away from Maxi, with his friends almost running to catch up with him.

"But . . . but you didn't answer my question," Maxi called after him.

BoBo didn't answer, either. Before Maxi could open his mouth again, BoBo and his friends had gone around the corner.

"What's the matter, Maxi?" a voice called. "Someone give you the cold shoulder?" Tony had come up behind Maxi with a couple of his friends.

"Oh, nothing much," Maxi answered. "I just asked BoBo if he is coming to Bible club tonight. Are you com . . ."

"Hey, Maxi," Tony broke in, "did you know that the Bilgewaters are on channel 13 tonight?"

"But . . . but you . . ."

Maxi didn't even get to finish his sentence before Tony had rushed his friends along the hallway. Maxi stood alone, watching Tony go the same way that Pookie and BoBo had gone.

Why . . . what . . . what's the matter? Maxi wondered.

That evening Maxi started down the street to Bible club but almost turned around to go home. *Who's going to be there?* he wondered. *Tony won't, and neither will Pookie or BoBo.*

But Maxi decided to go anyway. He wouldn't let the strange way his friends behaved keep him from going.

When Maxi opened the door, who should be sitting there but Pookie, BoBo, and Tony? Each one turned a little pink around the cheeks.

"Hi, Maxi," they all said together.

Pookie looked down at the floor.

BoBo sneezed and pretended he had to blow his nose.

Tony looked out the window.

Maxi said nothing except, "Hi," and sat down. He wanted to hear the club director's Bible story, which was about Paul's visit to Ephesus and the burning of the evil books.

"And do you know where those people came to burn their evil books? That's right, in the public place where all their non-Christian friends could see them. They weren't ashamed of being Christians."

Then the club director looked at Maxi, Pookie, BoBo, and Tony. "Have you ever been ashamed for your friends to know you read your Bible, or come to Bible club, or go to Sunday school?" he asked.

There was much coughing, sneezing, looking out the window, and looking down at the floor. No one wanted to say yes, and no one wanted to say no.

"I . . . I guess I was ashamed this afternoon," Pookie told Maxi after the meeting. "I'm sorry."

"Me, too," said BoBo.

"And me," added Tony. "Tell you what, why don't we each invite one friend to the club next week? OK?"

"OK!" all four friends said together.

LET'S TALK ABOUT THIS

What this story teaches: Jesus' friends should never be ashamed of Him, for we certainly do not want Him to be ashamed of us.

1. Look up Luke 9: 26 in your Bible. Read it together as a family. What would you think if Jesus were ashamed of you when you want to go into heaven?

2. What does Jesus think when we are ashamed of Him before our friends? Are you ever ashamed to tell others you are a Christian or that you read your Bible or go to Sunday school?

The Silversmith Riot

ACTS 19:23-41

Exciting things were happening in Ephesus. Paul preached daily about Jesus, and many accepted Him as their Savior. Some brought their evil books of magic and burned them where everyone could see. They were publicly telling all Ephesus that they had turned from their evil ways and were now following Jesus.

But all of this was hurting the silversmith business in Ephesus. Silversmiths made most of their money from the little silver statues of the goddess Diana that they molded. The people of Ephesus worshiped Diana, so they bought the silver statues to put in their homes. Visitors bought them, too, for many came to Ephesus to worship at Diana's beautiful temple.

Each time a person turned to Jesus, the silversmiths lost a buyer for their statues. At first it didn't matter, for there were only a few who had turned to Jesus. But as time went on, more and more believed in Him.

The silversmiths were now worried. Demetrius, one of their leaders, must have been most upset when he saw his friends and neighbors burning their evil books of magic. He knew that meant trouble for his business, and he made great riches in his work.

One day Demetrius called a meeting to talk with the other silversmiths. "You know that this is the way we make our money," he told the other silversmiths. "But this man Paul is telling people that the gods that we make are not gods at all. If this keeps up, we will be forced out of business, and Diana will no longer be worshiped."

The other silversmiths grew angry as Demetrius talked. "Great is Diana of the Ephesians!" they shouted. They shouted louder and louder, and others joined them until it seemed that the whole city of Ephesus was shouting.

A crowd formed, and some people grabbed two of Paul's friends and dragged them to the large open theater. One man named Alexander tried to talk to the crowd, but the people shouted for two hours without stopping. Alexander gave up and sat down.

Then the mayor of Ephesus stood up. At last the crowd became quiet to listen to him.

"People of Ephesus, we all know that Ephesus is the place where all the world comes to worship Diana," he began. "So why are you excited? These men have done nothing wrong. If they have, let Demetrius and his friends take them to court. If you think something is wrong, you should tell the city council."

The people listened carefully to the mayor. They began to wonder why they were shouting. They really didn't have a complaint. They were shouting only because others were shouting.

"If you keep this up, the Roman government will demand a reason for the riot," the mayor continued. "Then what will we tell them? Now let's all go home."

The silversmith riot was over. But Paul knew that it was time for him to leave Ephesus or there would be more trouble, and he did not want to make things hard for his friends in Ephesus.

So the Christians of Ephesus said good-bye to Paul. But they knew that wherever he went, others would come to know Jesus as Savior. So they must have prayed that the Lord would work through Paul in other places as He had in Ephesus.

WHAT DO YOU THINK?

1. What caused the silversmiths to stir up the people against Paul and his friends?

2. Why did so many people in Ephesus turn to Jesus? What caused them to do that? If someone asked you to describe Paul's work for Jesus, what would you say?

Sir William Double Trouble

"Call out the royal trumpeter," said King Maxi one day. "I have good news. I want to become friends with my people and give good gifts to them. Invite them to a royal feast at my castle."

"That's such good news that the people might not believe him," said the royal trumpeter, Sir Pookie.

"You heard King Maxi," said Princess Mini. "Saddle your royal horse and take the good news to all the kingdom."

"Yes, your highness," said Sir Pookie. "I will sound my royal trumpet far and wide."

Sir Pookie mounted the royal horse and went far and wide, sounding the royal trumpet. "Good news! Good news!" he proclaimed. "King Maxi invites you to his royal castle to dine with him and become his friends. He also will give good gifts to you."

The people gathered around Sir Pookie to hear the good news. It was such good news that they could hardly believe it.

"It's a trick, that's what it is," shouted a voice from the crowd.

"Sir William Double Trouble," shouted Sir Pookie. "Are you trying to stir up trouble for your king when he is trying to give you good gifts and become your friend?"

"A trick," shouted Sir William again. "Don't believe it."

Many of the people believed Sir William instead of the king's messenger. "A trick," they whispered. Then they went home instead of going to the king's castle to become his friends.

But a few of the people believed the king's messenger, the royal trumpeter. They believed the king's good news and went to the royal castle to dine with the king.

What a royal feast it was! The king met each person and became a friend. And he gave a royal gift to each one who had come to his castle because of the good news.

When those people came home, they told their neighbors about the royal feast and the king who had become their friend. They told also about the royal gifts.

"It's a trick! You'll see," Sir William Double Trouble insisted. "You'll be sorry that you went. Just wait and see!"

"No, the king is our friend," the royal guests insisted. "We know this is true. He has even given us royal gifts."

But most of their friends and neighbors listened to Sir William instead. They refused to be friends with the king. And they refused to go to him to receive his gifts.

After that the royal guests often accepted the king's gifts and talked with him. They became his good friends. Any they lived happily ever after, in spite of Sir William Double Trouble and all his suspicious friends.

LET'S TALK ABOUT THIS

What this story teaches: When good news is given, there are those who believe and live happily with it, and there are those who refuse to accept it.

1. What is the good news that Jesus brought? How was the good news in this story like Jesus' good news?
2. How was the way people responded to King Maxi's good news like the way people respond to Jesus' good news? What have you done with Jesus' good news? Have you accepted it so as to live happily for ever after?

Mini's Word List

Twelve words that all Minis and Maxis want to know:

BELIEVERS—People who accept what the Bible says is true because God caused men to write it. Because they accept what the Bible says, they also accept Jesus as Savior, for that is what the Bible tells us to do.

DEMONS—Evil spirits who live in people and cause them to do strange things. There seemed to be more demons in Jesus' time, perhaps to cause Him trouble.

FAITH—Believing in something, especially God, enough to affect the way we live. When we have faith in God, we try to think, speak, and act in ways that please Him.

HIGH PRIEST—In Israel, he was the priest over all other priests. He could do the work of a priest, but he also had his own work, which other priests could not do.

ISRAELITES—People who descended from Jacob, whose other name was Israel. Jacob had twelve sons, so all Israelites descended through one of those twelve men.

LOST—A lost person cannot find the way home. A person who is lost spiritually has not found the way to God. When someone helps that person find the way to God through Jesus, we say the lost person is found, or "saved."

PARABLES—A story that teaches something, for it has a second meaning. Jesus told parables, which to strangers seemed like only interesting stories, but to His followers they taught about God and His kingdom.

PHARAOH—A name given to Egyptian kings. It actually meant "A Great House," in much the way modern newspersons speak of news from the American president as news from "the White House." Actually the pharaoh was the whole government of Egypt, not just a person in the government.

PRAYER—Talking with God. We may thank God, praise Him, or honor Him as we talk, or we may ask Him to help us or others. We do not pray just to get things but to come to know God better and know what He wants us to do.

SAVIOR—A name for Jesus, for He saves us, or rescues us, from our sin. Jesus' death was an offering for our sin.

SCRIBES—In stories about Jesus, the scribes were men who had studied the law that God gave Moses on Mount Sinai. They knew much about that law and sometimes thought they knew more than they did.

SHEEPFOLD—A place, such as a pen, where sheep are kept. Sometimes it is called a fold.